FLOW

Santa Fe River Poems

Cynthia West

INKED
WINGBEAT

SANTA FE

*The Santa Fe River, that I've walked
almost daily through all the seasons,
is my friend, my mentor, my muse
and my inspiration.*

To her I owe many of these poems.

ISBN: 979-8-218-54096-8

Printed in Santa Fe, New Mexico

Also by Cynthia West:

For Beauty Way, Poems, Inked Wingbeat, 1990
1000 Stone Buddhas, Inked Wingbeat, 1993
Rainbringer, Poems, Sunstone Press, 2004
The New Sun, Sunstone Press, 2007
The Seasons of Tea, Inked Wingbeat, Blurb, 2010
In the Center of the Field, Poems, Sunstone Press, 2011
A Clear Drop, Poems, Sunstone Press, 2015
Visionary Paintings, Inked Wingbeat, Blurb, 2019
Seed Keepers, Poems, Sunstone Press, 2023

Cover Photo by Reno Myerson, 2024
Author Photo by Jerry Courvoisier
Book Design by Michael Motley

CONTENTS

INTRODUCTION

For some years Cynthia West walked through the low door-
way into the small Zendo on Cerro Gordo Road in Santa
Fe, just down the street from her home near the river, and
joined our Open Way Sangha in the practice of meditation.
When we finished, she would stand in silence, mindfully
unfold a piece of white paper from her pocket, and read one
of her poems to us. Then, she would bow and leave quietly.
I was awed, as we all were, into deeper silence, as her poems
led us even further down the path—a clear reflection of our
practice. The nature of our minds, the heart of the matter.

Through my direct experience, I came to see Cynthia
West as a kind of Zen master. A visionary who sees *what is*.
Her poems invite us into the natural world where life hap-
pens and death is part of life. Where birds stand sentinel
and the wind blows our perceptions open. Her poetry gives
expression to the cycles and seasons, the rising and fall-
ing of life on Earth. She is pointing to the breath between
words, the light that shines on what is, the seed as it ripens.
The spirit of that which is beyond concept. She knows these
things from her deep observation and her full participation
in life. As a painter she sees beyond the veil, as a poet she
speaks to what she sees.

Over the years, Cynthia has continued to share her
poems with us each week. No longer meeting in person, we
now meet online. Our Open Way Sangha has become the
Gaia Mandala Global Healing Community. Her poems travel
around the world virtually, and feed our prayers for global
healing and collective awakening with the spirit of nature
she reminds us to remember.

We need this reminder. It is medicine for us now. These are holy words, dusted in corn pollen, and sprinkled on the land. These poems carry the energy of awakened wisdom, lived through and through, walked into her bones and humbly offered to us. Her words echo the flow of nature and bring us back to our true self. Her vision expands our awareness, opening our minds to all that is. She is a great teacher.

Yet Cynthia West is a humble woman of simple ways, a woman of prayer, her pure heart and vision of basic goodness, grounded in the natural world. Her poems speak to what is truly important. We are invited into an ongoing ceremony in relationship with the unfolding of life on Earth, that we may remember our inseparability from the sun, the moon, the stars and the land that sustains us. In her words, we hear the drumbeat of the seasons, the old rhythm of mountains and rivers, the ravens who bless the corn in their sky dance. As her life, so fully lived, draws to a close, she offers us a full round of seasons to bring us into wholeness.

This book is an offering to our broken world. May we receive the teachings. They are "roses ringing with late summer," timeless stones, the river's music to our ears. Let us celebrate her life and what she has given us: that which restores our connection to each other and the world.

You who read these pages, hold a treasure in your two hands.

Cynthia Jurs
Guiding Teacher, Gaia Mandala Sangha
Founder, Alliance for the Earth
Author, Summoned by the Earth

THE PLACES BETWEEN

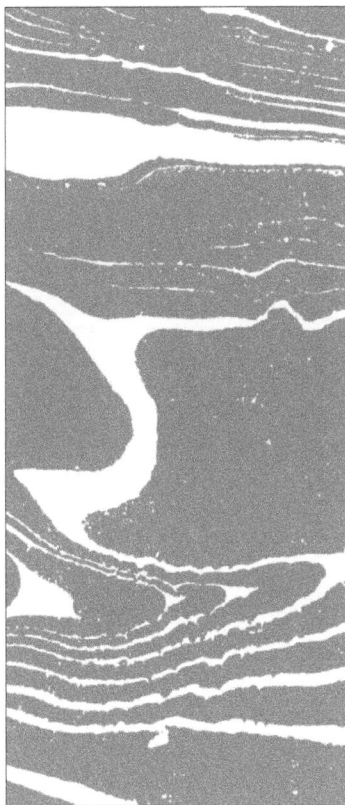

Early Winter

AWAITING WINTER SOLSTICE

A heron and a crane wait
knee deep in black silk water,
wings closed around them,
listening for the mountain to appear.

Rooted in the center of the earth,
the old birds have always
stood sentinel. Two long-legged reflections
slide into view beneath them
as dawn warms in the east.

Upside down in the still ripples,
they flow together, apart,
mingled, keeping the vigil,
calling the first light of the rising year.

They have fished for the sun
since time began, side by side,
blue feathers, white feathers,
bodies above, mirrored below,
silent as the mountain, the sky.

Grown old with the stones,
they stand, friends with the rain,
the trees and the falcons.

Their flute-like beaks sing
wind songs learned from the clouds,
a humming invocation,
a bridge welcoming the sun
to shine through their ancient eyes.

A NAMELESS MEANING

The places between are what matters.
    In early dark, snow settles
    on the fields. Bird tracks mark paths

to seed-weighted grasses.
    No winds whisper.
    The silence of rabbits in burrows

answers the sleeping hills.
    A nameless meaning slides toward dusk.
    The world is broken

in so many ways,
    there are cracks
    beneath every stone.

 Altars along the frozen river
    offer leaf rot and twigs.
    Mere shadows open doors,

allowing furry creatures
    to find their way
    through ice-tangled boughs,

into the night, quiet
    as the clouds loosing snow.
    The places between are what matters.

THE DRUMS MEET

Calling in the night,
    your voice searches dreams

for the nameless seed
    of yourself.

It can't split open until
    you become as quiet as air,

as still as the frozen river.
    It can't sprout

until you travel
    through deep fertile dark.

Merging your body drum
    with the rhythm

of the wheels beyond time,
    stirs sap to ascend

through roots forming leaves.
    Energy flows up,

a thousand wings
    restoring broken promises.

SHINING IT BACK

Cliffs weep when darkness
    swallows the earth in its maw.
    Dry grasses raise tiny faces -

seed heads with eyes waiting
    to open. Patches of snow hold
    tears frozen between blinks.

Touched by silver rays, the cedars
    sigh back and forth with the moon.
    Friendship speaks rivers,

one water mingling with another,
    sharing meanings that vanish
    at the touch of thought.

Turtle-faced snow clouds flying
    from the west are wise
    with the secret sun's return.

Frozen stones slide long shadows
    under the edge of night.
    The cold has many faces,

some clear as ice receiving
    sunlight, shining it back.
    Friendship speaks rivers.

THE QUIET ROOM

When our walls cracked
   and I no longer knew
   how to hold them up,
   I rose in the dark
   to sit in the quiet room.

The trees grew tall,
   with branches sheltering
   the stone steps that lead to peace.

Aloneness first brought me here
   to light candles
   for your gentle touch.
The full moon shone,
   a silver ocean breathing in and out.

Traveling mountains
   that weren't on any maps,
   I met myself dreaming.

After gathering twigs,
   kindling fires, heating pure water,
   I am ready
   to offer you tea.

Nothing is here but our empty bowl
   and our bow in the quiet room.

THE SMELL OF WARM BREAD

The tyranny of time robs our days,
leaching gladness. It dams the river
of meaning that dances us all.

Trapped in patterns of minutes
that are never enough,
our bones have worn thin

rushing up the rungs of ladders.
Without time for the laughter shared
around tables of good food, we forget

the smell of bread fresh from the oven.
Without trust in the moment,
we're shadows who can't remember

how to ring the bells of our senses
as long and loud as we want.
It's lonely in the winter

when we no longer know how to fly
with the swallows, how to sway
with the wind blown trees.

ROADS DRAWN ON PAPER

Fleeing the ruined earth,
   we didn't realize the roads
   drawn on paper would become
   our walking trails.

Crimson clouds ride
   dark December skies
   illuminating the canyons
   we marked with stones
   on our maps to the next world.

We didn't guess the springs
   we imagined would offer
   pure water to our thirst.

Breath by breath
   we uncover presents
   planted long-ago in dreams.
In the dark of winter,
   with the earth sunk in silence,
   we inhabit the rooms,
   the arches and vistas,
   the pathways and havens
   we believed into form.

EDGELESS

Our bodies contain spirits
    dancing with the wind.
Loosed from limits,
    we weave our days
    into egg shaped houses,
    each with a door
    opening to the sun.

Our thoughts are sea birds
    free to dip and soar.
Playing with the waves
    since before time, our laughter echoes
    with salt savor, crashing into rocks,
    cresting joyous foam.

The fences we worked hard
    to maintain are falling down.
Under smiling stars,
    we are meeting, holding hands.
Beyond the hellos and goodbyes
    that bound us in separate sorrows,
    one moon reflects in still water.

WHEN WINTER IS DEEP

1.

One moment you are sweeping
the front porch, the next,
caught up in a flock of stellar jays
circling the hillside across the road,
you rise, swift wings beating
in cadence with hundreds.
All you know is the sound of air
through feathers,
the language of speed.

When the wind sings you weightless,
you soar the blue beyond blue,
merging with the hillside,
the cedars, the stones.

2.

One moment you are gathering moons
in a dream, rowing rippled reflections.
Luminosity clears your ears to hear
the green sounds roots hum
to each other when winter is deep.

Fishers of light inhabit you
with a long, bright path passed down
in the songs of giant pines
rooted at the center of the world.

THE REMNANT

Out in the dust of what once was
a blue lake, we are the remnant,
the ones who have embraced
the stranger inside
who can't be killed by change.

We are the ones who have broken
the habit of avoiding what matters most.
Tears, memories and beliefs
have blown away in a climate
gone mad from abuse.

Out here, where no one wants to be,
we have the peace to look up,
weaving sun-motes and wonder
into roads never seen.

We are learning how to restring
our guitars with the silence
found between stones.
We are discovering
how to polish our trumpets
with feathers dropped by hawks.

Patched instruments, we play
the best we can. Even new born sounds
weave nests where
miracles can lay eggs.

HIDDEN RIPPLES

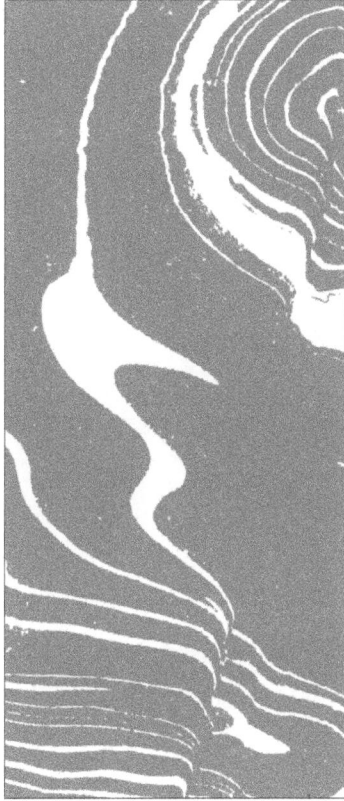

Late Winter

THE BEAUTY ROAD

The earth is a house of paintings
   waiting to be translated
   onto canvas, paper, stones.

Walking the beauty road for years,
   you have caught visions
   before they could fly, nourished them
   with the milk of your heart,
   touched and been touched in return.

Leaving a trail of images,
   you reach land's end,
   the shore and the sea. The journey
   has taken so long, it is night.

Along the way, you left most
   of what you brought, shoes, clothes,
   beliefs, easel, brushes, colors.

A full moon rises over the horizon,
   casting a silver ladder to your feet.
Stepping on the shining bridge,
   enter between
   what appears and disappears.

ALONG THE PAINTING ROAD

It's been pretty good,
not knowing of how my brush will land,
or which winter hour will open time.

Without face or name, I ride
each painting until it sings.

Imperfection unlocks doors.
Between just right and off balance

rests an altar of discovery,
a space for new breath.

The membranes separating
everything vanish in snow.
A sun dog radiates on clouds.

Because I left my eyes along the way,
they can't be burned
by too much light.

WHEN MANY SEE

Your open sight
   sparks the dawn into flame.
   When many see,
   the water hidden under ice
   awakens earth from sleep.

Join the rhythms
   of the long nights' breath.
In the presence
   of all who have passed,
   dance the old circles.

Wear the evergreens
   of eternal life. Weave your threads
   into the patterns
   on the red cloak of knowing.
Open a road the light can follow
   into the shrines of hearts.

Heed the voices
   that never stop. Whirl with the poles
   that unfold the unknown.
   There is no way
   to stop beating together.

A RIPPLING MOMENTUM

No amount of trying   will allow you to become
         the river
               as it laughs downstream.
Only when you give up,
        asking the water to let you
        enter its changing flow,
  will it whisper secrets.

If you submerge your head,
        the current washes
            your ears clean
  to receive what your mind
  cannot contain.

In the river you are golden silk
        carrying clouds
           on your back,
  a rippling momentum
    with no end.
You're a moment   that disappears,
  a fountain
    of racing leaves,
  fluid and solid merged,
    leaping over stones.

Folding in and out of yourself
        dancing
  with the stars beyond time,
        you have learned how to arrive
  by leaving.

FORWARD MOVEMENT

The sky is a giant wing, its upswing,
   a brilliance the eyes can't bear,
   its downswing, a death shadow.
Hearts know this rhythm
   because it is their own.

The steady pulse clears vision
   until every pebble shines
   as if viewed through pure water.

Threatened, then illumined,
   we grope along a narrow road.
Light, dark, light, dark, repeat faster
   than we can breathe.

Wearing nothing but the wind,
   our flesh, blood and bones
   join a forward flow
   learned in hidden dreams.

Cloud walking, we remember
   dancing beneath the surface
   of the mind.

Moving the body within the body,
   we're a river of gentle lightning,
   scaling ridge-lines
   beyond the end of the world.

WINTER WEAVING

A stranger, unknown as a country
that has never been mapped,
walks frozen river banks,
asking the silenced water song
for her true name. Winter weaving

is too quiet to answer,
but inside the snow a story stirs.
The red bowl of her womb,
painted with rainbows and lightning,
is a cave warming her seed.

Birds find shelter here,
teaching her songs she remembers.
Their voices are roads leading
to dreams lost along the way.
Their wings are hands
joining the pieces whole.

Warbling ripples restore the face
she hid beneath the ice, allowing
her to arrive in the inside house,
where she dwelt as a child,
before she forgot. The birds

hold her here, eyes and mouth closed,
sprouting with the light
that can't be seen,
washed by the waters of beginning.

THE LISTENING PLACE

When it is too late for anything
    but releasing fear
    and letting it flow downstream,
    it is possible to merge
        with the current under ice.

In the listening place,
    we learn stories older than thought.
Freezing waves restore
    us to childhood, rippling,
    at home with our family
    of reflected clouds.

Roots joined in the center
    of the earth, we sing
        with trees and stars.
Washed clean, we dance our way
    to the great crossing.
Raising wings skilled
    in passing over,
        we await the call.

IN THE HOUSE OF WINTER

Ice blossoms crown cherry boughs,
   each a flute calling silver birds
   to chime. Crested Jays hop piñons,
   wings beating snowflakes.

Silent arms enfold the valley
   in the house of winter.
White as the hills and fields,
   we offer sky-soaring chants,
   gathered from the pure cold,
   woven with the breath of clouds.

We're singing to complete our gifts
   for you, the hidden earth,
   for you, the heart of the waters,
   for you, the fire within the atom,
   for you, the unseen air.
Our voices are snow, showering
   gratitude down on you.

Echoes are all we leave,
   soon to be erased.

STARTING OVER

Tonight we dive down
to the center, once again
gathering the sand grains
with which we formed the planet.

Sleek, furry, fast and whiskered,
we find the way even though
it's been longer than memory
since we were last asked
to renew the earth.

We have been told to bring up
the tiny cells of beginning,
to blow on them kindling life,
to plant them in the wreckage,
as we did before.

Looking like wet rats,
tending the fires that don't go out,
we're moon ripples, murmuring
with the loons and winds.

Diving through water deeper than longing,
our small paws reach
into the spirit belly of the world,
asking to be given new seeds.
We are the ones
who know how to plant.

PLANTERS OF DREAMS

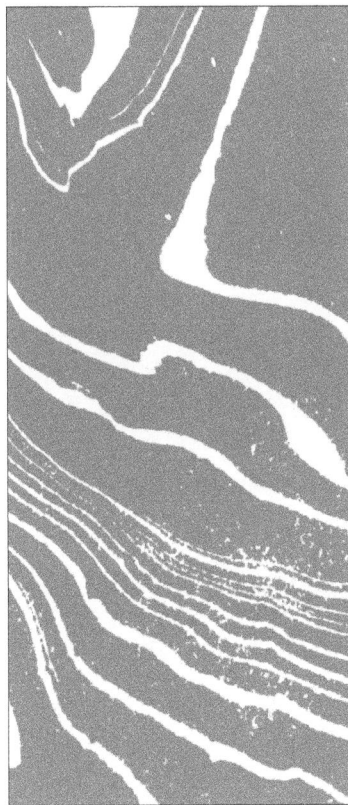

Early Spring

PLANTERS OF DREAMS

When the road beneath our feet
   is blowing away,
   we offer importance to the sky,

finding friendship among the clouds.
   Quiet ears hear the mountain's roots
   singing with old stone voices.

Simpler than feathers floating,
   we are gatherers of gifts.
   No longer you and I,

but the spaces between branches
   joined in a wind-swift circle.
   Breathing inside moments,

we open the melodies
   that turn the wheels beyond time.
   Planters of dreams, tending seeds,

there is no waiting as we melt
   with the snow-clad peaks
   into green beginnings.

THE RIPPLING SPRING RIVER

We appear overnight,
    a crowd of green grasses,
    neither sure where we have come from,
    nor certain where we are.

Finding bravery in numbers,
    we share dreams,
    riding the river with cloud reflections,
    tossing sun sparks back and forth.

Being here together strengthens us
    to grow, roots entwined,
    playing liquid melodies.

This hour and day we dance
    in all the sun we ever wanted.
Breathing in the sweet smell of sap,
    we're much larger than we thought.

THE RAVEN'S EYE

The secret to climbing into spring
   is not carrying much stuff.

You will only be allowed to stay
   if you are open,
   without ideas and words.

When you no longer
   have to have your own way,
   the raven's eye will admit you.

The blackness will not be closed,
   but a door to the river's voice,
   almost too soft to be heard.

When high winds polish
   your emptiness,
   you ripple, transparent
   in green leaf veins.

Cottonwoods bend and sway,
   finding space
   to sing through you.

GIVE THEM THE CHANCE

You are a transparent doorway
    for dreams to enter the world.
    Leaping, laughing, fighting,

consuming, reproducing,
    irrepressible energies
    thank you for giving passage

to the gifts they offer.
    If you're not wide open,
    watch out, or they will seek

a more welcoming host.
    Bow when you see them near.
    Offer them your emptied self.

Stand back. Thank them
    for planting your bare earth
    with seeds that root, bud

and leaf green wonder.
    Stand back. Thank them
    for choosing you.

ONE LISTENING FLOW

Warm, soft moonlight floods
   your head and body, leading you
   to follow silver dreams
   out to ride the river
   until the voice of water
   becomes your own.

With no words, windows,
   doors or walls, your feet
   are peace sinking through ripples
   - no difference,
   just one listening flow.

With no face, no name,
   you learn the river language
   that smooths stones,
   that reflects bright clouds and leaves.

You are a free floating force
   infusing roots with colors,
   a sun-flashed current dancing.

Fluid, fast, you're way beyond
   what you thought
   you had to be.

SONG OF THE ROAD

Old family photos
   - we never looked satisfied.
   Young, healthy, gifted,
     we didn't know
     how to be who we were.

Decades of wandering
   wore us smooth as stones
   in a river-bed.
     The road taught us to accept,

to grow in trust,
   opening our red centers
     to drink the sun.

Vulnerable
   as new-hatched finches
   feathered at our mothers' breasts,
   we learned
     the song of the wind.

Dancing with clear waters,
   we entered the heartbeats
     of rivers and trees.

A RIVER OF CERTAINTIES

Walking out of the mirror,
    a flickering reflection, follow
    the messages that beat
    in your blood.

Above cottonwoods waving
    incandescent green, the sky opens,
    receiving you into
    a river of certainties
    deeper than the mind.
In the house of your eye,
    every glance feeds many.

Energy creates family trees,
    singing, dancing branches
    for colorful birds to nest.

Going in and out
    of the house of the eye,
    you form mountains, canyons,
    waterfalls, stars and moons.

You populate deserts
    with fur, feathers,
    scales and howls. You cultivate
    fields of flowers and fruit.

No longer inside the mirror,
    you share feasts and laughter
    under shady boughs
    in the valley as it was
    when the earth was whole.

BALANCING

To Drury Spurlock

Friendship is wet stones
    balanced on tiny points
    standing in a river of snow melt.
    The combination of shapes and weights
    holds together
    despite water rushing on all sides.

We're learning how to build
    with our sharing. One smile
    anchors the next, unfurling
    new green leaves
    in the dark cold.

Our various aspects form a structure
    where each kindness
    is supported by the one before
    while providing
    a foothold for the next.

Companionship looks
    as if it's bound to topple,
    yet, stable in the racing flood,
    it holds steady for no reason
    but our balancing
    each moment of wonder
    with the one before.

SPINNING A CIRCLE

The walk you came to complete
   is a song path weaving voices
   on the loom of the unseen.

Give thanks that your river flows
   no matter how many
   stones block the way.

The masked weaver bird gathers
   grass stalks to form a new nest,
   grieving all that is lost.

Bright and dark strands
   pulse from your drum.
   With no time for regrets,

shining threads raise
   a circle of forgiveness
   from the ashes of the old.

Wearing bright new flesh
   woven from tears,
   you're learning

to dance
   with the unknown.

THE PRAYER ROAD

You've been so busy
    your house is piled high
    with unfinished prayers.
Yes, they are windows, and yes,
    winter has passed.

Go out. Follow the trail
    that disappears up the cliff.
It is littered with gifts broken
    by your lack of attention.

Tell your legs they are strong.
It is too late for anything but
    offering all your water
    to the earth that gives life.

With fingers gripping ledges,
    scale lichened rocks,
    shelters for eagles.
Up here in strong wind,
    your feet remember
    the way past the damage
    caused by thinking
    you were right.

Don't pretend to forget
    the path through the clouds.
Use grief for your mistakes as fuel.
The sheer red stone is flesh,
    beating with your heart
    until the two balance
    in the understanding that each step
    toward the sun forges a path
    for many to follow.

The prayers you offer
    are open doors, welcoming
    those you've never met
    to enter the true face.

The face is the same as yours,
    as theirs, as the cliffs', as the rivers',
    the one face since the beginning,
    the one that always is.

ASTONISHED WITH BELONGING

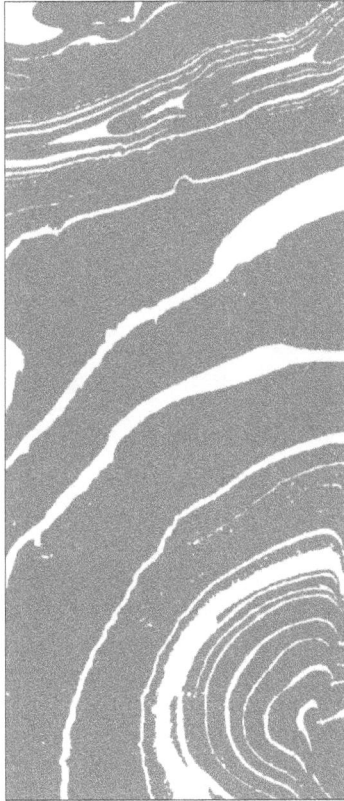

Late Spring

THE LARD CAN LID

I found a rusted, round lid
   along the road, brought it home.
   It was the top of a five gallon can,
   hauled up Cerro Gordo from town
   on a horse drawn wagon long ago.

Lard was a staple in every household.
   The emptied tubs were dumped in the arroyo.
   Decades of sun, wind and hail gnawed
   the metal reddish brown,
   with ragged holes in places.

As worn and thrown-away as I,
   the lid taught from where I left it on the porch.
   Showing nothing is lost by being ruined,
   it soothed my fear of growing old.

Ordinary, drab at first glance,
   a closer look told the canyon's story
   of snows, floods, droughts,
   the years of piñon covered hills,
   the circling moon, the dawn light,
   the dark of winter.

An ancient magic mirror, its plain surface
   opened the doors of my eyes
   to the prayers stones hum after rain,
   to the chants of high-winging hawks,
   to the quiet of deer nibbling wild verbena.

ON TURQUOISE MOUNTAIN

Used to appearances,
   I accepted small days

until horse clouds
   galloped me beyond
   the world of people.

Years on Turquoise Mountain
   emptied me

until I could no longer hide
   from the sky, the rain, the earth,
   the sun or the moon.

I am a thousand eyes,
   no different from the air.

You wonder why
   I'm up here alone,

laughing in my little house.
   I can't express

how the wind
   blows me apart

only to put me
   together again.

THE VIEW IS TURNING

Clouds, shadows and branches
    drop clues luring you
    to reach past skin, beyond bones,
    to touch the essence
    inside the appearance,
    the nothing
    that holds everything in its hands.

Patience has years of seeking.
One step after another in the dust,
    pathways lead to water.

Hand and eye never stop probing
    the changing shapes, now here,
    now gone, now flesh, now ghosts.
Subtle hints flash in and out of form,
    quicker than loss or gain.

Blown here and there,
    you coax the tree within the tree
    to show its face. Quicker than you,
    the view is turning,
    spinning in and out of reach.

DREAM WOMAN

Playing in the water,
    I launch yellow leaf boats
    loaded with wishes for the river
    to wash to the place where
    dream woman's fingers form
    beings from clay.

She weaves the golden water
    into passageways between us,
    conduits to transport my requests
    into her rippling hands.

Examining my wet prayer wings,
    she skims off sticks and twigs,
    polishing the seed within my pod
    to sprout green leaves.

Reaching out, she plants my tree
    in her completeness
    where my colors laugh and cry,
    astonished with belonging.

THE WIND WILL CARRY US

The swallows taught us to gather mud,
    to form it into dwellings.
In our earthen villages we dance,
    we sing, begging forgiveness
    for the harm we have caused.

We question hawks, deer, coyotes –
    how can we put ourselves right
    before the wind blows us away?

Each morning the sunrise swallows us
    until there is nothing left
    but the call of the mourning dove.

We plant circles
    of corn, beans, sunflowers,
    trusting they will ripen
    before the wind blows us away.

SPRING PLANTING TIME

Digging beneath your face in the mirror,
    there are many layers,
    colors of joys, sorrows, mistakes.
Ready the ground to receive
    the seeds patience saved.

Let the smiles of clouds
    strengthen you to delve
    through lost friendships,
    wounds left by closing doors.

Water drops on dandelions carry sun sparks.
Catch and hold that primal fire
    to sprout your dreams.

Lie flat in the river,
    begging release from the traps
    you set to stop
your wild body from running free.

Here in the digging down time,
    with the wind howling dust,
    there is not a second to lose.

Grow a bountiful tree
    whose shade is forgiveness,
    whose branches are simplicity,
    whose bark the woodpeckers fill
    with secret songs.

OUR LAST MEETING

to Asha

With feet born of faith
   we walk arm in arm,
   listening to the calls of bluebirds
   in cedar boughs,
   following the songs of clouds.
Friends on the flower road,
   we ride the wind
   that carries the mind to silence.

We know how to scale cliffs
   where rain whips rocky ledges.
We don't stop on the way
   to the caves where bells ring.
The green tempest has blown
   our seed stars away,
   until, as with dandelions,
   only our cores remain,
   brighter than the sun
   with shared laughter.

Together today, our hands
   encircle one another. The orchards
   witness our farewell,
   more apples than we can count.

When we first met,
   we knew we would always
   nourish each other with loaves.
Our smiles would share honey
   after our bodies left the earth.

TO ASHA

In Memoriam to Asha Greer

Asha, Asha, sister,
    in the vast silence you opened
    for our roses to drink,
    you wake,
    more alive than ever.

In a plain pine box,
    buried on a frozen hill in Virginia,
    you have lost all limits.
No longer restrained from being
    everywhere, you cavort in and out
    of the hundreds who love you.

Asha, Asha, sister,
    in the winter ice
    you are the new earth
    wearing a huge golden dress
    woven from our hearts.
Transparent as the dawn,
    you are a mountain
    full of roots that can dance.

The morning glory skies
    your arms wrap around our sorrows
    ring blueness beyond sound.
Flocks of your prayers wheel free,
    winged shapes in the sky
    that dive, pouring peace.

Asha, Asha, sister,
    your friendship is the pure water
    you heated to serve us tea,
    the medicine you offered all.

Your care continues to warm our bellies,
    soothing the empty aches,
    growing the trees you planted.
On new wings you travel
    to all our countries,
    gathering us into one body
    smiling above the mud.

Asha, Asha, sister,
    gazing skyward, joining
    your great song,
    we shield our eyes
    from the brightness
    you are shining down.

ENDLESS BLUE TUNE

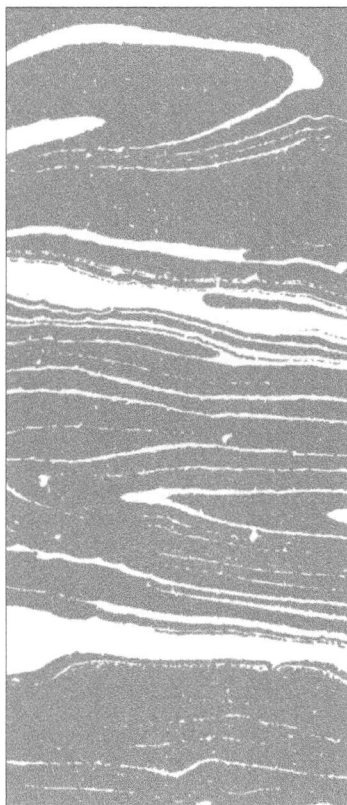

Early Summer

THE BOOK OF THE MOON

Memory does not live in time,
    nor will it allow dreams to surface
    before they are ready. Lunar beams
    define what brought you to this valley.
Hold the knowing in your fingers,
    urge it to stretch its wings, take flight.

It guides you, as it does the clouds,
    the swooping swallows,
    the black beetle in the dust,
    the wild gourd vines.
It offers you the confidence
    of stalks bearing corn,
    of rustling growth in shade.

Let the moon be your eyes,
    your hands, your skin, your bones.
Let the moon be your tongue drinking
    the gift too deep to be found,
    too close to be named.

Outlined in silver,
    follow the singing water
    the book of the moon
    spreads beneath your feet.

UNDERGROUND CAVES

Rabbits scamper across the field
    with the moon on their backs,
    showing us where to start digging.
    They grant permission to carve paths
    where we were told not to go.

With hands and stones we tunnel
    into underground caves,
    shelters where soft clay holds
    the tales we're here to uncover,
    the circles our feet danced
    long ago, when we were whole
    among our people.

Feathers we tied to sticks
    asking the clouds for mercy,
    still deliver our prayers.

When the water inside water
    beats the first drums, our hearts,
    the hidden river of our voices joins
    with hummingbirds and marigolds.

Bison and deer taught us,
    when we were young enough to listen,
    of the flame in the seeds
    we first carried from the sun.

BEYOND THE SECRET

For years, we bowed,
   asking to learn
   the pathways out of limitation,
   into the wide family
   beyond the horizon.

We screamed for release
   from the fear that bound us,
   one problem after another.

Only when we gave up,
   sobbing in the dust,
   did our brothers and sisters,
   the gentle winds
   stroke our cheeks.

Only then, did Mother Earth
   re-form our bones
   with sounds that merged us
   into the new pulse,
   the one beyond the secret.

Now that the sands
   we thought we could hold
   have run through our fingers,
   we're clouds racing across the sky,
   white wings past understanding.

DOVE WINGS CLAPPING

Sweeping fear from my threshold,
   I step out to join the moon choir,

the sound of countless dove wings
   clapping hope throughout the canyon.

My dreaming house, lit by colors
   from the insides of my eyes,

has windows allowing views beyond
   the chaos gnawing at foundations.

I'm still dancing in the rooms
   I painted with radiance

mixed from healing waters
   and flower petals' tears.

Hummingbirds fly through the ceiling,
   opening pathways for the stars

to pour kindness into possibilities
   waiting dormant in cocoons.

THE SAME FLOW

Women pray, kneading dough
   on floured tables with strong,
   capable hands. Pulling,
   pushing, activating yeast.
Bread comes alive under
   their motion, the repetitive flow
   of streams nourishing valleys.

Old, aproned women rock
   back and forth,
   the same as giving birth,
   as making love, as mourning.
Bodies voice the rhythm
   in baking, planting, harvesting,
   in raising children, building families.

Daily sweeping the yard is prayer.
   As if circling sacred sites,
   they take out the garbage,
   wash the dishes over and over,
   scrub fingerprints off the door.

Women pray, kneading dough
   on floured tables with strong,
   capable hands. Pulling,
   pushing, activating yeast.
Bread comes alive under
   their motion, the repetitive flow
   of nourishing streams.

IN THE ORCHARD

to James McGrath

A laughing bird among
    horsetails and grasses, you walk out
    of the kitchen door, carrying food
    to guests in the orchard.

Magpies, robins and crows
    merge their dreams with yours,
    for they know you
    are a keeper of the river's voice.

Passing years weave circles,
    one into the next,
    a choir of penstemons and wild plums.

The book of water gathered
    by your deep listening to friends
    opens truths to bloom.

Fulfilling the patience of years,
    you kneel on the earth, cultivating
    each sprout, no matter how small.

You form a bridge between people,
    plants, rabbits and birds, for all to pass
    under the wing of thunder,
    offering the one big song.

WE ARE THE SAME

to Jason Alexander

Since I don't know where you are,
    I imagine us standing
    on the bridge over the river
    under green-arched leaves.

Magpies gather in the canyon,
    squawking complaints.
    You may dream of their harsh voices
    shaking down apricots.

Although you are far away,
    I feel you here, right beside me
    in the cool shade, enjoying the ravens
    sipping sun-flashed ripples.
    Small, round clouds that tell of rain
    fill our sky with wonder.

On the familiar road,
    picking winged seeds from trees,
    we are the same as when
    you were learning
    how to walk. Holding hands,
    we skipped, singing a little song.

Just as then, there is no distance
    between us humming
    along the summer day
    on the path to the waterfall.

BEYOND WINDS

Winds are hands that reach
    through the skin to deliver wounds or healing.
    Some swim in the current beyond thought.
Some knock on closed doors,
    coaxing them open.

When wise winds vanish, baring
    the grief they concealed,
you face the ache
    of not receiving what is yours.

When you're vulnerable
    from missing the boat
    with your name painted on the side,
    the path collapses under your feet.

When you forget
    the power winds have over you,
    and quit thinking,
    you rest in gentle clouds.

When you fall silent,
    love blooms wider than the sky,
    friends with the great winds
    breathing beyond time.

YOUR GATHERING BASKET

Gather clouds on the edge
   of appearing and disappearing.
   Trust the place
   in between being and not.

It takes patience to watch
   your basket fill and empty
   without trying to hold
   what you thought was yours.

It takes acceptance to walk
   the sunflower road carrying
   what seems to be nothing,
   then seems to be something.

Your heart is a basket,
   receiving impressions
   of water dancing corn to fullness,
   of pears blushing ripe.

Tiptoe – listen with all your ears
   to the quiet in your basket.
   The roses' song
   may let itself be heard.

It opens petaled doorways
   so you can find your path
   though the winds of change.

ENDLESS BLUE TUNE

Sometimes you need to look with your ears
    to see the road you've traveled
    turn to gold in the late sun.

Sometimes you need the sky
    to swallow you gently, rather than
    giving you tasks beyond your skill.

Sometimes you need to bow
    into the spaces between your cells
    until limits melt
    into the endless blue tune
    you remember cooing as a child.

Sometimes the earth reaches into you
    with hands that touch the fire
    you brought when you were born,
    the spark that quickly hid
    in the rush and roar of days.

Sometimes truth is kindled,
    restoring your voice to mingle
    with the river of sound
    that carries all life.

Sometimes, remembering,
    your own eyes recognize who you are,
    the one you never believed,
    the one, who, looking out,
    can see the road.

SHARING THE RAINBOW

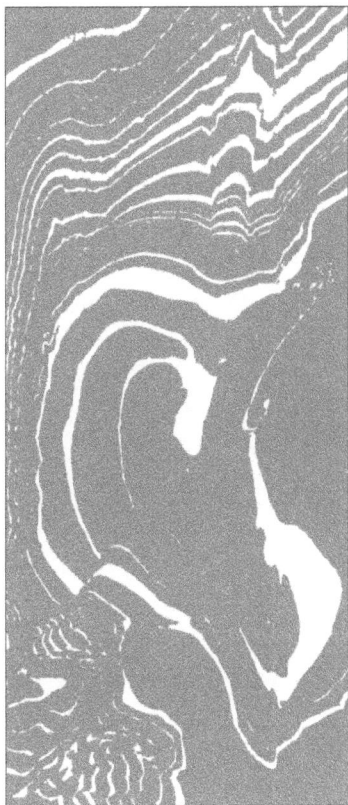

Late Summer

A FEW FRIENDS

There are no tourist stops
    on this road. Those who can't love

    have stayed back, snapping photos
    of sights, stuffing trinkets in bags.

A few of us friends continue,
    hearts torn open.

No longer able to hoard treasure,
    we water the way with tears.

Each letting go provides
    a new fullness of breath.

Light as the moon's reflection,
    we float whole, forgetting

    the grief of false promises,
    shining

    with no need
    to make sense.

ROSH HASHANAH

What will be
    hides in the new moon.
    The next story hasn't yet
    revolved into view.

Your body, shadowed as well,
    is a tree with birds sleeping.
 What will be waits for you
    to kneel in the silence
    between dark and dawn,
    a silhouette before
    the blue of beginning.

You are a listening chamber
    resounding with the chants
    that started the world.
Timeless songs ring the edge
    of hearing, shadows
    rippling down-river.

What will be is blue birds
    birthed out of passing clouds.
Circling, they generate winds
    that fill your new eyes with light.

A PLACE LIKE THAT

1.

Where do butterflies rest
   when they no longer swoop
   through marigolds?
   Is there a place like that for us?
Where are their songs
   that we never knew we heard?
After our bones return to earth,
   is there a shelter
   for our quick-winged minds,
   a river to soothe our loss?

2.

Above, among the cottonwoods,
   crows teach their children
   stories they will need to survive.
   The young ones will continue
   the dawn watch, passing light
   from one to the next.

3.

We and the roses drop seeds
   to bloom our kind forward.
We join the deer, the rabbits,
   the eagles, every beating creature
   who doesn't fear
   time is too short.
Like the butterflies,
   we don't want to be anything
   but what we are,
   without questioning
   what could happen next.

ABLE TO HOLD

My red clay body,
    kneaded, spun on the wheel,
    fired in the kiln,
served many until anger
    smashed it to pieces.

In the sunflower field,
    the moon enters my prayer
    teaching me to restore
    the vessel I've ruined.

It leads me to gather
    the shattered parts
    and fit them together,
allowing rainwater
    to smooth rough edges
    until they can no longer cut.

It tells me, broken bodies,
    when joined together with love,
become treasure vases,
    able to sing beyond form.

Able to enter the dawn's wings
    and to hold each other,
    just as the mountain's arms
    shelter the greening fields.

DEPARTURE GATE

This body is a waiting room
    for flights departing
    to lands with names
    only in heart language.

Ceilings of back-lit butterfly wings
    shelter chambers ready
    to turn tears into gold.
Dreams lie stored here,
    awaiting activation.

If you have left your baggage
    in the terminal,
    listen for the the flight
    to your next lesson.
At the gate, present your ticket.
Be welcomed aboard.

Down at your old address,
    dear ones will mourn
    as they box up your things.
It will rain.
The seasons will turn.

GENTLE WINDS

The seeing that reaches beyond form
    is in our small eyes so we can know
    the house we inhabit
    is larger than the stars.

Petals are doorways
    into flowers that never fade.
    Gentle winds unravel the knots
    we've built to protect our hearts.

No need to regret
    doors rusted shut from mistakes.
    Water cleans harm
    too quietly to be thanked.

Grape clusters hang heavy,
    calling our prayers
    to eat their fill so they can fly
    spreading friendship.

Clouds leave footsteps on lakes
    for us to follow.
Walking the fluid skin,
    we are sunlit water.

We are bells, pears and roses
    ringing with late summer.

OUR DAYS ARE SHORT

We green-breasted hummingbirds
   swill pea blossom nectar,
   storing fuel for a six thousand mile flight.
The wind will carry us from the known
   over oceans and towering pines.

Our little bodies are fading
   under the autumn sun.
Our coats are worn, our shoes
   as well. The paths we thought
   went where we wanted
   have led to grief.

With little left of the garden,
   we are grateful
   for lizards scurrying up the path.

Like hollyhocks going to seed,
   we weep bittersweet parting,
   as we say farewell.

Flying strange skies, we will sing
   of the loves we have left.
We will strum the wind's feathers
   until our wings grow strong
   for the flights beyond.

EACH SINGING QUILL

Before you can paint the oriole
    she vanishes in a summer cloud.
The silence of her absence
    is bigger than all your colors.
Starting with blues floating in and out,
    your brush probes through
    to the other side of the canvas
    where the bird of sunlight flies.

Her wings drop feathers in the garden,
    knowing you will arrange them
    to express friendship.
Spreading spaces between each singing quill,
    evokes an inaudible hum.

With her under-wing down
    that sways in still breezes, you gather
    the moments in between moments,
    the colors inside colors,
    weaving musical threads
    only the inside ear can hear.

You and the oriole sing with one voice,
    no sound, no color, only the warmth
    of sharing the rainbow
    after it has hidden in the sky.

THE GATE OF CHANGE

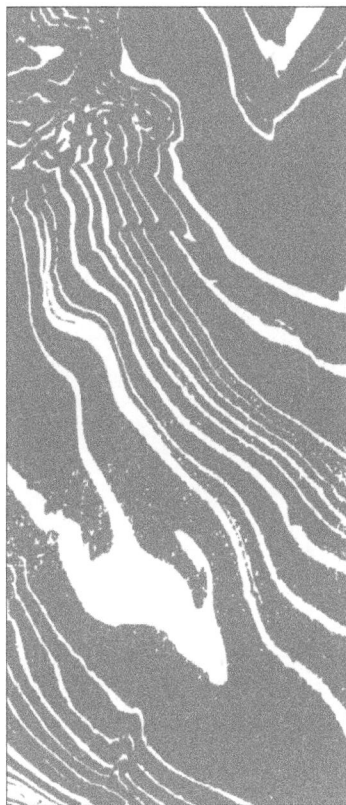

Early Fall

LISTEN NOW

On this first day of fall we forget
that those who lived in the valley before
are still present. Startled by
a sudden movement, we glimpse
a shadow as it slips away.

Until we understand
the sighs of wind-blown dust,
we won't hear the long-ago children
laughing and playing games.
We won't feel the weddings
or funerals in the apple orchards.

Because we're listening,
we hear their spirits
sliding through the piñons.
We sense those who loved
the round-backed hill in the north,
who harvested the silence
of the south, who rejoiced
in the west wind's song,
who shone with the dawn.
Their peach trees in the arroyos
still bear wild fruit.

Joining them and the crickets
on warm autumn nights,
we form a choir sounding rhythms
that restore the way it was
before the people took too much.

THE RIVER THAT BROUGHT ME

If you wonder where I come from,
look at faded photos
of someone who wasn't me
but rather, a patchwork of parent's hopes.
Those who imagined I was their child
were yellowish days
that tasted heavy in the mouth.

Those who didn't know how
to join the dances that circle
the sun inside of seeds,
insisted I act out
their limited scripts.

With only dreams for shelter
there was nothing but to let the wind
chase me across sand dunes
following the tracks
of mournful gulls.

As I dug on the shoreline
with a small, wooden trowel,
trying to get back to the river
that brought me, waves
washed forward, erasing my path.

Gathering shells with small holes
I hoped to build a necklace
that would serve as a bridge
to lost wholeness,
if only I had enough thread.

ASKING SWALLOWS

They needed me
  to be like them,

stealing each other's smiles,
  collecting them in stacks,

painting them gold
  with sarcastic laughter.

But I was asking
  swooping swallows

to teach me how to settle
  by tall cliffs. How to follow

the sun and moon
  across the sky. How to live

with the patient stones
  in light that makes me weep.

WHAT IS ASKED

It is hard to learn what is asked,
to find what we always run after.

Becoming water is the only way
to enter the rainbow, leaving our bodies

begging by the roadside,
swallowed in light.

All the rights and wrongs
will continue, just as before.

We will forget our understanding,
just as before.

Strange, how the morning
joins and separates,

how no trying can keep it together,
how the rainbow can never be held.

It is hard to learn what is asked,
to find what we always run after.

THE GROUND SHAKES

Bells clang with the fury of dark hoofs.
The ground shakes under the weight
of the galloping cold. Bare branches
tremble,
weaving snow clouds into dreams.

Veins quiver, filled with doubt
among the ruins left by taking
more than we should.
When earth's protective veil
is torn, her round shoulders
submit to burial in snow.

Winds sweep beliefs away
until the air cries, heavy
with lost confidence.
Cold hearts can't beat fast enough
to kindle memories
of how to start a fire.

Using every ounce of faith
to remain standing
in the gale of change,
we dare to spread
our last seeds,
with no assurance
they will survive.

WHAT MEANS MOST

When cold breathes
down the mountain,
casting snow on the peaks,
it's time to light the first fire.

When golden leaves are borne away
on wind horses' backs,
emptiness opens,
spreading our wings wide.

Dahlias bow frost-blackened heads,
murmuring regrets. Roots pulse,
slowing to rest.

What means most inhabits
the loneliness left
by the absence of growth.

There is a still space in loss
for truth to awaken.
Wisdom woven underground
rises up our bones,
replacing frozen flowers
with voices of belonging.

The river inside our bodies
makes itself heard. It doesn't matter
if the view is locked in ice.
Our warm veins
are silent gardens flowing.

PAST THE LIMITS

Yellow leaves surrender,
  casting glory with the winds
  only to be blown to mud.
Beyond the need for beauty,
  they don't fear the loss
  of golden moments.

Under skies bluer than truth
  there is no being in control.
The whole cycle, from birth,
  to leaf, to death, vanishes
  in the freedom of release.

The river pulsing through all
  is the same water
  since the very beginning.

Before people forgot,
  they turned on the sacred wheel,
  singing and dancing,
  honoring primal flows.

Drink from the current inside you.
It is the force that knows
  when it is time for the branch
  to release your one last leaf.

THIS AND THAT

There is no need to walk alone
    in a strange country
    when your own lilies
    welcome your presence.

There is no need to leave *this*
    for some of *that*.
Every moment breathes
    a thousand meanings.
Every view offers layers of wonder.
The garden of dreams
    pours in clear windows.

Your body is earth,
    mapped with rainbows holding
    red mountains. Blue oceans are here
    and grape vines watered by tears.
The sky is alive with clouds
    raining roses' smiles.

This home teaches how to walk,
    how to breathe,
    how to not pretend.
This is a magic box opening
    to freedom every day.

PICKING BEANS

As dusk fades to brown,
an old woman bends,
filling her basket
with scarlet runner beans.

Alone, under storm clouds
blowing from the west,
she listens to autumn sighing
in the voices of dried vines.

One song mourns
green leaves released.
Another rattles yellow farewells
to the cooling earth.

In the grief of sinking
toward completion,
she accepts she too has had
her time to flower, to seed.

Dried pods, the same as she,
hide rows of shining
promises
to grow another year.

DARK NOVEMBER MOON

Under the dark November moon
    there are circles of ashes in the field,
    hours of sharing, gone,
    heart flowers watered with tears.

Dry gourd vine, red root and pigweed
    tangle over graves. Here lie the barks
    of dogs long gone. Here rest the echoes
    of bells that ring no more.

The swollen taste of death remains
    on the tongue long after naked trees
    have borne witness to our loss.
Pain, grown dull, remains.
As we sit in the distance of years,
    the needle of today
    sews fabric over memories.

Loss is a dark purple flute played
    by the wind. Ravens gathered
    on branches welcome empty sky,
    talking the language without hands,
    the coldness river stones speak.
Black beetle's tiny feet measure
    the distance between grains of bone.

RABBIT TRACKS

Searching all those years
did I ever look
into my own eyes?
Only rabbit tracks remain
across the snowy field.

BREAD FOR YOU

Golden leaves toll the sinking light,
   leaving little time to give you
   all I've harvested.

Those years you thought me gone,
   I was weaving flowers into blankets
   to warm your shoulders
   on long winter nights.

Stitched with stories,
   they whisper comfort
   when you are alone with the stars.
Enjoy eating the bread,
   baked with the corn we grew.

Here are my worn shoes.
Let them protect your feet
   from today's changing roads.

Here are the dawns I gathered
   while asking for songs
   to soothe your sorrow.
Tasting the melodies,
   your mouth will open,
   freeing praise birds to soar.

Visit the stones I've set in circles.
Desert shrines are places to drink
   the wonder that satisfies thirst.

As golden leaves release,
    befriend the moons
     who taught me to create.

Here are my paintings, my poems,
    your guides
     as the world falls apart.

My home is now yours.
Years of adobe bricks,
    laid one upon another,
    hold you in peace,
    speaking the language
    of mountains and birds.

THE BRIDGE WITH WORN PLANKS

Some of the boards in the bridge
    feel they could break underfoot.
You stand, unconcerned
    you might fall in,
    for you already flow
    where dreams lie waiting.

Overhead, crows speak patterns
    your nerves understand,
    a braille for lost people.
Vanishing into the sound,
    you read the promises left concealed
    on the undersides of boughs.

No words are needed in the silence
    when your face meets itself
    in the center of the sun.

The river that sweeps through you
    is your own true water, not the theater
    you thought of as yourself.

Leaping over stones, the light
    whispers, asking you to carry it
    to both sides of the river.
The bridge with worn planks
    will support your steps.

NO TIME LEFT FOR DOUBT

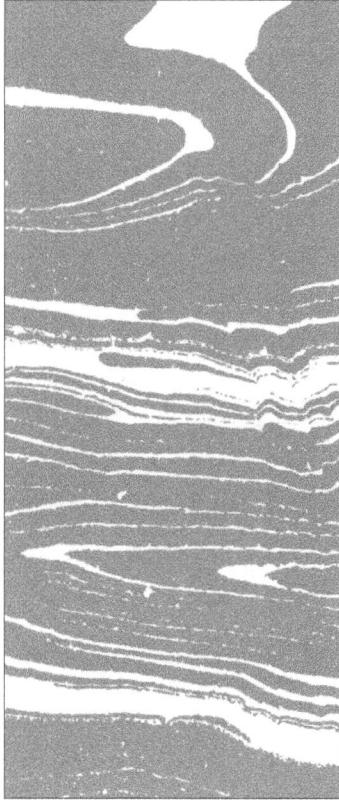

Late Fall

WHAT YOU BROUGHT WITH YOU

Detours through mountains
    were given before you arrived.
Grow strong scaling the boulders
    where eagles nest.
Wear whispering clouds until
    you can no longer find yourself.

Listen to the wounds
    you brought with you
    teaching that what is,
    is alright.

As dusk falls, the birds
    of your broken promises
    are building warm nests.

Don't be concerned about
    how to tell the stories ice gives.
Sharing, you will be filled
    with new omens.

Climbing the road that allows
    no stopping, no rest,
    grows the feathers needed
    to bridge the chasms ahead.

Most of your weight
    has been spent.
With no time left for doubt,
    leap off any cliff. The wind,
    knowing you, will carry your body
    to the next impossible test.

SKIN WORN THIN

Acting in dream theaters
distracted me from mirroring
the emptiness of clouds
flying over snowy peaks.

I pulled out my eyes,
borrowed against them
for the sight that can enter
the doorway to nothing.

I sold my feet to the false promise
that good deeds
would carry me past
my shaking reflection
into the land beyond grief.

My clothes were traded in the hope
they could buy me time.

With skin worn thin by the wind
I am quiet enough to enter
the moment that opens
only to those who are small.

WHAT KIND OF BIRD

the stone cold sky speaks
water on the edge of snow
what kind of bird
am I wet feathers
afraid to cry

caught in an oil spill
full of mud and death
black wings vanish
in the empty night
even stars weep

a hawk chased by ravens
across wind blown clouds
can I race faster
than the thousand fears
threatening this day

thinking I'm not a bird
replaces the sky on my wing tips
with locked doors
no more breath
salty tears falling

I'm a secret bird
working in the still of night
where the moon
will not notice
my feathered face

NEVER AT HOME

We can't recall what stopped us
    traveling from here to there,
    strangers never at home.
    As the moon phased full to lean,
    our eyes couldn't find the horizon
    or a place to rest.

Maps pierced with pins marked places
    that meant nothing. Foot prints
    were washed from the sand
    as if they'd never been.

We gathered our broken pieces,
    bits of green glass,
    fragments of shells,
    remembered pebbles.

We stuffed our bags with withered flowers,
    skeletons of mice caught between stones,
    butterfly wings deprived of flight.

We hauled useless souvenirs
    back to the mountain as if they could
    return us to wholeness. Unpacking
    in winter wind, we cried,
    smelling the freedom we had lost.

THE URGES OF MOTHS

Birthed by darkness,
propelled to become light,

flying bullet bodies
crash into the window.

Many die on impact,
patterned wings tumbling

among fallen leaves.
No one notices the tiny ones

in frozen mud,
crushed from crazy want.

We sleep, unaware
of their heroic impetus

to re-enter the stardust
from which they were born.

A GARDEN DANCING

For a little hour
    I've been a garden dancing,
    a page in your colored book.
You tended my seed
    in your house of paintings, raising it
    to join many-colored flowers.

With singing sunshine you watered
    my roots to grow through stone.
Shaping my heart with petals,
    you made me a green summer,
    a child of the moon's melodies
    at home with the stars' vast smiles.

Raising mountains for me
    to grow upon, you shaded
    my leaves with friends.

Knowing the painting will not last,
    I've hurried to add beauty,
    brushstrokes gathered
    in wonder and despair.
Pigments I've mixed from jewels
    mingle with your work.

You give and you will take,
    first blotting out my light
    with ink ground from twigs burned black,
    then changing me into a new earth,
    one with balanced light and shade.

For a little hour
    I've been a garden dancing,
    a page in your colored book.

ON *SEED KEEPERS* ...

"Your book of poetry [Seed Keepers] is blowing my heart/ mind/spirit wide open and causing me to feel admiration of your courage, skill and eloquence as an offering of medicine that's pure and beautiful as all your transmissions have been. Many thanks."
   — Nina Simons, co-founder of Bioneers
      author of *Nature, Culture and the Sacred*

"I stayed up late one night last week reading your poems in Seed Keepers. *Thank you. They are terrific. I especially love the ones where you get spunky, ie, "To My Doctors." And, of course, the cover is gorgeous! Congratulations!"*
   — Natalie Goldberg
      author of *Writing Down the Bones* and *Wild Mind*

Seed Keepers is available from Sunstone Press
sunstonepress.com

ACKNOWLEGMENTS

My thanks go to the following publications, events and people:

"The Beauty Road," Grand Prize, Artist's Embassy International, Dancing Poetry Festival, 2021

"To Choose and Combine," First Prize, Artist's Embassy International, Dancing Poetry Festival, 2021

"Rabbit Tracks," Gusts #36, a Tanka Journal, 2022

"The Lard Can Lid," *New Mexico Poetry Anthology*, 2022

I'm grateful to Able West for his patient willingness to correct revision after revision. Collaboration with poet friends James McGrath and Morgan Farley provided invaluable support and inspiration.

What means most in the act of creating is the faith and encouragement of friends and family. I can never thank Cynthia Jurs enough, author of *Summoned by The Earth*, for posting my work weekly to her international circle.

I would also like to thank my husband Reno, Mark Myerson, for giving me the time and space needed to express the inexpressible. Without the enthusiasm of Jai Lakshman, James McGrath, Valerie Tibbetts, Walter Nelson, Jesse Law and many others, this book would not have come to fruition.

An immense amount of gratitude is also due to Michael Motley whose design and production skills have elevated the quality of this volume.

Last but not least, many thanks are due to Michael Smith, "The River Man" for transforming large stretches of the Santa Fe River Corridor from a dusty tangle into a beautiful park. Simply because he cares, on many days, he can be seen weeding, pruning, planting, clearing and raking. After many years, his largely unrewarded work has created a restorative natural refuge that inspires dog walkers, visitors and wandering poets.